MAKE AMERICA *Laugh* AGAIN

The Comically Incorrect Cartoons of

of

ANTONIO F. BRANCO

VOLUME TWO

A.F. BRANCO ART
BURLINGTON, WASHINGTON

Make America Laugh Again
The Comically Incorrect Cartoons of Antonio F. Branco
Volume Two

Published by:

    A.F. BRANCO ART
    P.O. Box 992
    Burlington, WA 98233

ISBN: 978-1-5323-8008-2

Cover and interior layout design by Lovelace9Design, LLC

Printed in the United States of America.

In Dedication

To my mother, Audrey — Your unwavering support for all the things
I have passion for. Your unconditional love and kindness are not overlooked or underappreciated.
I hope you know how much I love you.

Proverbs 31:25-30

In Memory

To my father, Tony, Sr. — Your ability to think critically, your wit, and your
common sense have been an inspiration throughout my life.
You would have loved this book.
You are missed.

Exodus 20:12

ABOUT THE *Author*

A.F. Branco was born and raised in Mendocino County, California, and later relocating to Northwest Washington state.

Branco served in the U.S. Army MP Corps, which offered him the opportunity to attend college on the GI bill.

He is a talented musician — plays guitar, bass, and sings — who, with his band, "Tony and the Tigers," played gigs all over the Northwest.

Over the years Branco created cartoons as a hobby, until he saw America under assault by radical Leftists. Then the hobby became a calling and another form of service to the country he loves and swore to protect from "all enemies foreign and domestic."

Tony's 'toons resonate and inform and do so with razor sharp humor, accruing a following of patriots everywhere.

Branco has appeared on Fox News, the Larry Elder Radio Show, the Lars Larson Radio Show, and more.

A.F. Branco's first book, *Comically Incorrect: A Collection of Politically-Incorrect Comics* — Volume 1 (November 2015) was well received. His calendars sell out each year as the demand for humorous cartoons increases in an otherwise mean-spirited political climate.

And now, with *Make America Laugh Again*, A.F Branco continues slaying the dragons of Leftist Lunacy via the power of the cartoonist's pencil.

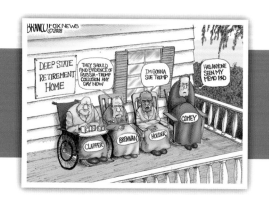

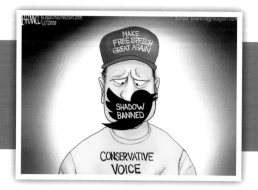

FOREWORD by Tami Jackson

Some people seem to know their calling from birth. Others happen upon it via a meandering path in life. Either way, figuring out what you were born to do is a very good thing.

A.F. "Tony" Branco meandered, first serving in the Army MP Corps, then attending college on the GI Bill, then working at a sawmill in Washington state.

All the while Tony paid attention to what was happening in politics and culture, translating events, and even folks in the workplace, into humorous cartoons.

But as our country began veering sharply to the left under the "leadership" of Barack Obama, Tony decided to take his cartoons to the next level: from hobby to actual job. After all, America the Beautiful was under assault, he felt called to do something.

Tony has a gift: his cartoons force even die-hard curmudgeons to crack a smile, and often burst out in laughter. What commentators and others do with sharp rhetoric and repartee, Tony does with his pencil.

Ah the stealth method of communicating and informing via cartoons, especially A.F. Branco cartoons! In laughter folks learn about the reckless destruction of Obama, the underhandedness of Hillary Clinton, the utter ridiculousness of thin-skinned snowflakes, the Progressive purpose of Mainstream Media, and more.

People everywhere recognize "Branco" toons, and share and re-tweet at will.

All these years later, Tony did discover his calling, meandered back to serving his country: this time via cartoons that serve up a healthy portion of common sense and patriotism with a kick of reality.

The Republic needs artists, cartoonists, such as Tony.

Stay the course, my friend! Keep drawing truth and conservatism cloaked in your priceless humor!

Tami Jackson
2018

5

6

End of an Error

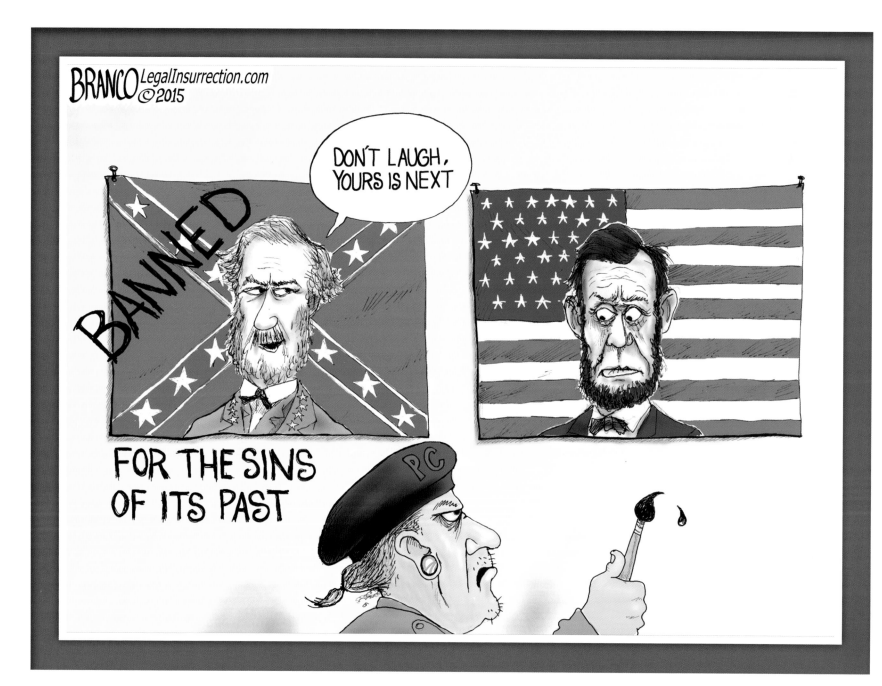

8

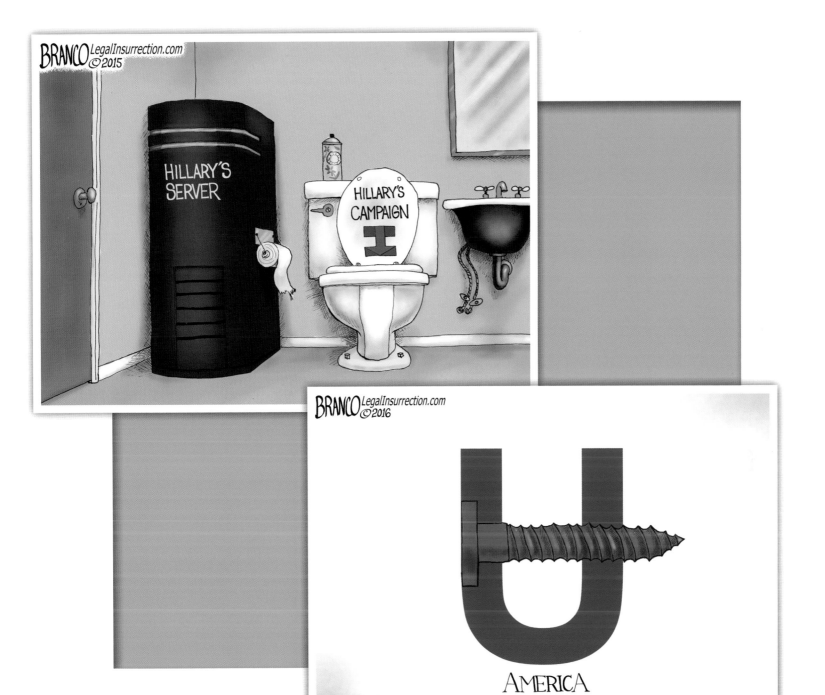

9

10

11

13

14

15

16

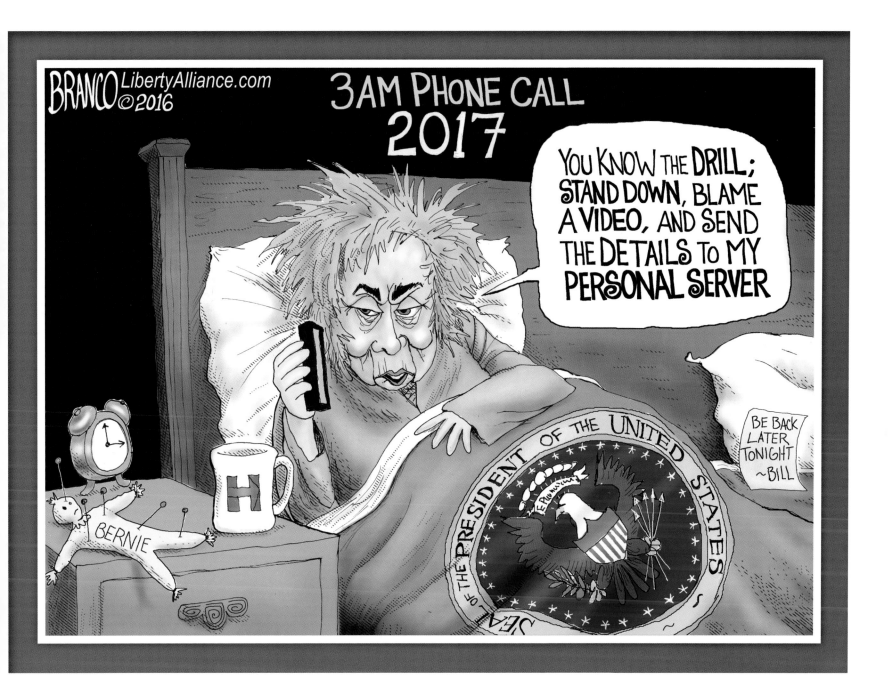

19

20

21

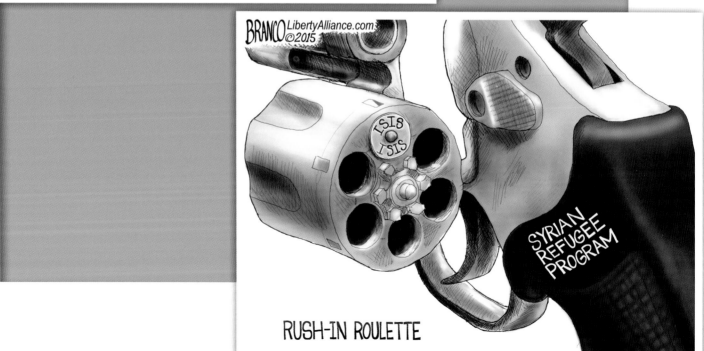

22

23

24

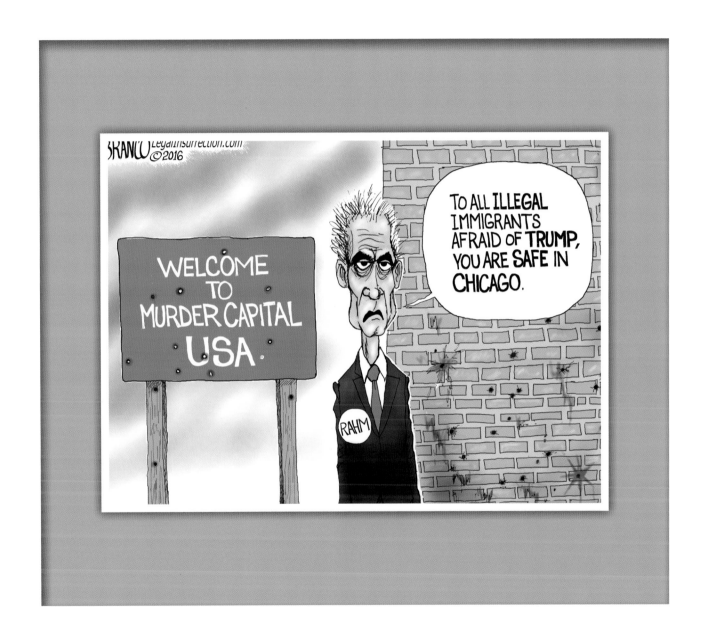

26

Making America Great

30

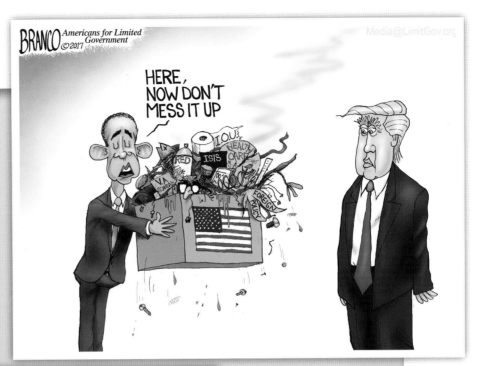

31

34

35

39

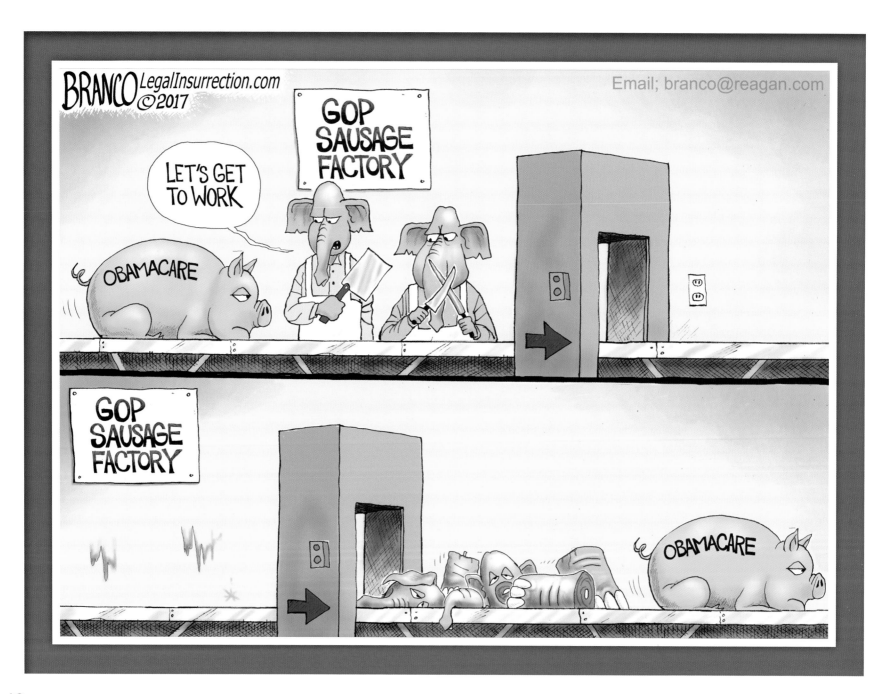

40

41

43

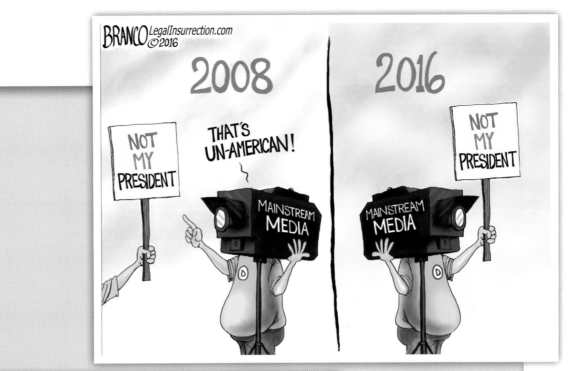

47

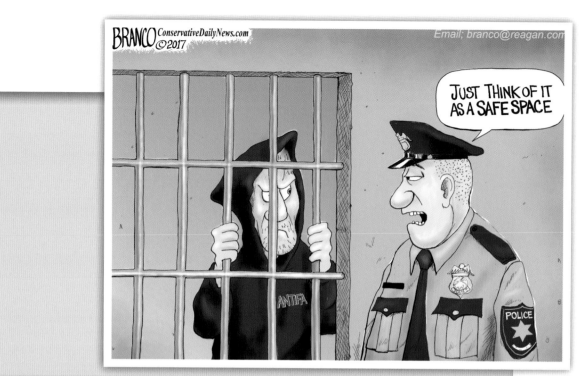

49

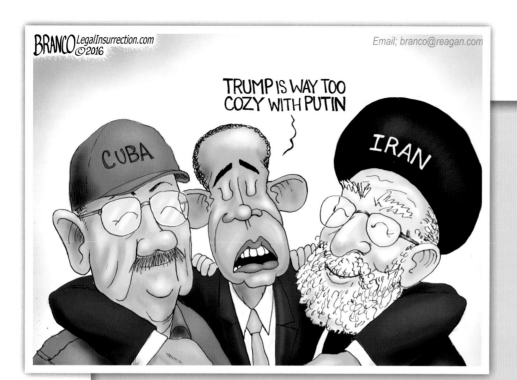

50

51

52

53

55

57

58

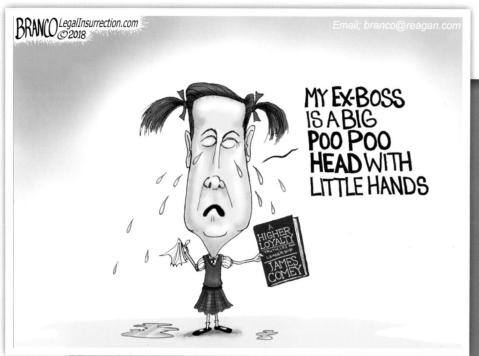

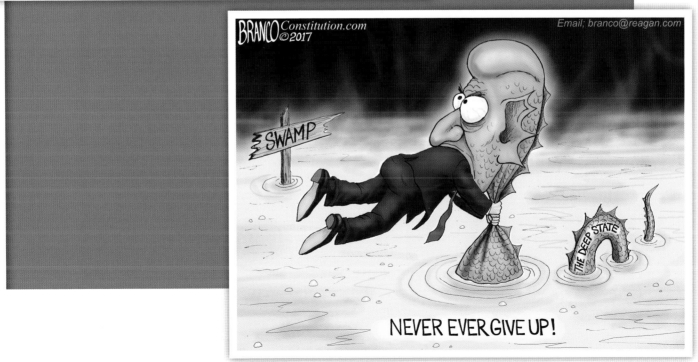

63

68

69

70

71

72

73

The End